AF447465

CLI
BOOKS

WILDFLOWER BLOOMING

WILDFLOWER BLOOMING

POEMS & PROSE POETRY
BY CRYSTAL REYES LOZANO

Wildflower Blooming
© 2024 Crystal Reyes
ISBN: 979-8-218-43622-3

First Edition, 2024

Printed in the United States of America

Edited by Nicole Gates
Cover Design by Annie Cercone
Layout Design by Jim Dodson

Self-published with the support of CLI Books

To the outcasts, the black sheep of the family, the ones breaking
generational curses, those who are different, *unique*.
Para los border kids, those chasing the American dream,
to the single moms, the survivors,
the in-between
to the life experiences that shattered me
&
the ones that inspired me to write.

For anyone who needs this book, these words, *estos consejos*,
these stories gained from living,
this is for *you*.

acknowledgments

Firstly, I want to give thanks to the universe, divine spirit, God; the energy that surrounds me & guides me.

Professor Josie- you opened up this world of creative writing & showed me how to treat writing as my own B-A-B-Y. You encouraged me to get out of my head and just write. Thank you for acknowledging a glimpse of my talent, I am eternally grateful.

A personal thank you to the writers in my community & the Community Literature Initiative (CLI season 10 family, ILY<3), who saw these verses firsthand & allowed me to share such vulnerable stories.

A BIG thank you to my circle of close & long-lasting friendships: Susie, Felix, Liz, Alejandro, Saul, Victor, Morgan/Erlan. We push one another to grow in a healthy stance, and y'all have kept me sane through it all. Thank you to my kiddos, Evelyn, Luna, & Enzo, for loving me in all the phases! I do this for you.

Un millón de gracias a mi otra mitad, Rafael, gracias por amarme y aceptarme por todo lo que soy. If it was not for you, I would not be where I am today. I love you, always <3<3<3<3<3

Muchas gracias a mis abuelos, for showering me con un amor incondicional. Este libro es para ustedes.

And finally, my dream team at work & my students that inspire me day by day, this is my legacy to the literary world.

table of contents

preface

Amores,

Oftentimes, identity, trauma, and familial issues are diminished within certain cultures. I wanted to make sure I touched on all the appropriate topics I happened to live through.

Many of these poems were crafted in the beginning of the pandemic. From scribbled towelettes from the local mom & pop shops we frequent, to the notes section of my phone, writing is always on my mind. This collection of poetry started off as squiggles and one-word ideas and has flourished into this epigraph of love notes. Rock bottom has served as a way into the vision of these written works, an internal voice that represents moments in my life, the light & the dark.

Estás palabras, are an oath to who I have been, who I am, & the person I am blooming into.

I hope you find connection in my journey

Content Warning
Self-Harm
Domestic Violence
Sexual Circumstances
Depression
Eating Disorders
&
Other potentially upsetting topics

Make sure to take proper care of your mental stability every day,
but even more on
the tough days.

hecha en México

my mother ran into alien arms
de un país a otro
walked in white down the aisle
took the body of Christ,
to be blessed in bloom
full-bodied, glowing in presence
i arrive early for the date
blanketed in fear
faintly yellow
so still & quiet
glass chamber cradles me

<u>silhouette</u>

|| the radiance of the sun becomes you
with that decadent smile,
where we walk for miles
you bring me happiness as

i become enchanted by your mesmerizing bliss
sea waves twinkle if they could see your eyes glow
the fragrance of your curls,
pierce me as i find myself in remembrance
with the beauty of your soul ||

<u>i used to wish i was a gringa</u>

complexion too pearly; most days i am white-passing
Spanish rolls off my tongue in swiveled sentences;
baila, baila, English dances perfectly

"[but] you don't look Mexican!" -again,
i am critiqued and ridiculed
papá an immigrant,
un conquistador, searching for the American dream

mamá probed him with infatuated love cues
i became the first love product; i played pretend
my dad's name is *Juan*, not John

i relinquish my Spanish self; *la mejor parte de mi*
i want long-straight hair,
not these springy spirals,
gracias mamá

distant resolve

tirada, sobre el piso, como ropa vieja

you glare at me, dignity down the drain

frozen by your stare, afraid of the next chapter

'where do I go from here?' i ask myself repeatedly

days turn to weeks, years fly by

    lies spit from the corner of your tongue, hot on her heels

    heavy on my mind, yet she is the one you were trying to find

did you ever really love me?

doble vida, nothing set and stone

        dejalo, libre.

        liberaté, you are more than these apologetic excuses

        now, where do i go from here?'

amargada

escuchas pero no entiendes,
dices que comprendes, pero cómo?
sí no aprendes

you give your two cents here, babble babble,
puro chisme de tú boca, sonreís para no hacerte la loca

madre eres todo y nada al mismo tiempo,
hot and cold you analyze and paralyze us with your spoken word

"mija por eso no adelgazas…"
yet you send me home with
conchas, gorditas, y todas las golosinas

sour then sweet,
me juzgas, y te burlas, de las cosas,
things that you have yet to comprehend;
old wounds left to mend

pandemic baby

para-Enzo

mask hugs my mouth, restricted airflow,

i wish for you, each monthly appointment, amid a city 'red alert'

strict orders from the doc, sign dangles from the door,

|NO spouses allowed|

i have a piece of you, i pocket them near me,

wrinkled, slimy seahorse, swiftly swimming

bloom & sprout month-by- month;

cómo pastelito relleno de mermelada

oven set at 350 degrees; swelled up tummy,

anxiously awaiting your arrival

viscerally nestled within me;

corazón latiendo con el mío….

<u>fuck depression</u>

clustered cotton-candy clouds / spiraled through the sky /

razor kisses my wrist / like uninvited men at the palm of my hand /

ruby rose droplets / trickle onto my pillow / *respira profundo* /

YOU are enough

southern summers

Desde niña, i grew fond of the bumpy, rocky roads of Montemorelos

we would reach our destination when a whiff of animal manure

the airspace and exhausted me of the fresh breeze

| drought, uneven patches of golden grass *cubriendo el rancho,*

my heart skipped a beat, ba bump, *mi burro awaiting me //*

el aroma of home-grown

tomatillos & jalapeños

would surround the outside porch

and my body would quiver from the prickle,

my abuela would heavily press down on the *molcajete //*

salsa verde chilaquiles were my favorite part of the morning |

México se convirtió en mi hogar

<u>morenita</u>

you are dark & you are beauty
    oscurita / bien bonita
    iridescent melanin

          vampira hispana
          el tiempo no te alcanza

no te crees hermosa / ni divina / ni diosa /
    moonlit golden goddess
        dancing delicacy
        in all your glory,
 this is YOUR story

me pinto los labios
para mi
no para ti

-@Crisreyeswrites

<u>skeletons in my closet</u>

never search for the secrets of someone,
unless they voluntarily give you permission
because then you will be left with a closet

full of their subconscious desires
&
those were meant to stay hidden,
for a reason

<u>smitten</u>

crinkled pewter strands of hair where turquoise once danced

our bodies bare, yet i am the only one who truly cares

your eyes whisper, 'i love you' over coffee

you don't wanna conform to the idea of us

/no holding hands\

no eye contact that lasts more than 8 seconds, psychologists say

"that's where true love lies"

yes, we agreed no fallin' in love

<u>vida a la Mexicana</u>

sobre las montañas de mi querido Monterrey,
my childhood spirit *vuela y gíra,*
entre el rancho de mis abuelos

vegetales a la orgánica,
leche del pezón de mi madre,
traditional norms that existed a mere five generations before me

machismo que nunca muere,

a voice of a woman drained and taken
so, it becomes as silent as communion in session,
on our usual Sunday mornings

cualquier queja de la mujer casada y si a caso se sobrepasan;
it is viewed as minimal as the tapping's on my windowpane
la vida es más allá de cocinar platillos of cuisine,
half-heartedly afforded, a combination of *arroz blanco y frijoles negros*
el platillo yin -yang le digo yo.

la vida es más que ir a la orilla del río, los Martes y Jueves,
para lavar la ropa a mano

cómo quisiera viajar más allá
de las cuatro paredes que van rodeándome a diario

<u>picture-perfect polaroid</u>

body contoured to the shadows of the lens

camera shouts at lightspeed

overexposed, your beauty bleeds

interwoven layers,

you & i

face forward flashing;

connectedness to the raw

narcissistic is his middle name

i was his puppet, he was my master
how could love become this whirlwind of disasters?

control
that's it
           his domineering self hit,
here we go again, gaslit

machismo was his ego
one that blinded me
           why, though?

subtle arguments,
ended with his hands at my throat
           if i did not oblige,
worst was yet to come

after the violence,
the emotional followed
           stabbing & jabbing,
these miniaturized holes that are never to heal...
so I can return to them and remember...
           what is left for him to steal?

−my heart continuously shattered

hush-hush

| *te amo en secreto,* where shadows lurch, obscurity lives,
donde nadie reconoce

mostly, in warm winters underneath the chimney
uttering sweet nothings, *cositas sin importancia*

away from the judgements
caught up in the giddy frisson of a new romance

confined to you, *la sociedad nos juzga*

you are a sinful habit, *que no quiero echar a perder* |

| *te amo en secreto,* where shadows lurch, obscurity lives,
donde nadie reconoce

<u>valle hermoso</u>

they call it, "beautiful valley"
broken city
topes por cada calle
niños in the family hustle
vendiendo chicles
struggling to make ends meet
hot-dogs a la Mexicana, tacos de fajita
basking in happiness with lukewarm food at their sight
remedios to fill shattered dreams
drug cartels run amok
santa muerte hangs from thy neck
tótem de magia
la familia, always first, never last
el gobierno, glorified savior,
                    absolve us

<u>quízas | maybe</u>

| *quizás, nuestra relación de un mes,* was not meant to last
after all, we were just teens
teens who knew nothing about what **"real"** life entails

quizás, no querías comprometerte con una estadounidense
an american who would eventually move back to the states
a girl who is too direct, too outspoken, *muy 'loca' para tus gustos*
tan 'loca' que ahora me buscas,
      ruegas por volver a verme, una vez más

maybe | quízas

| maybe, our one-month relationship, *no estaba destinado a durar*
después de todo, solo éramos adolescentes
adolescentes que no sabían nada sobre lo que implica la vida "real"

maybe, you didn't want to commit to an American
un estadounidense que eventualmente
regresaría a los Estados Unidos
una chica que es demasiado directa,
demasiado franca, too 'crazy' for your tastes,
so 'crazy' that now you look for me,

you beg to see me once again |

~~uninvited~~

| his trousers hit the floor,

he thrusts into me

with unnecessary atrocity,

        no invitation…

        no welcome sign…

        no blooming flowers…

    just the echo of my screams fighting back his inner demon

        i lay there, deadly corpse,

        alienated from the flatline of my emotions

        the exasperated moan he exhaled was all

        that it took

            to put a halt on his action |

i was too afraid to walk away…

-soledad

grandfather of mine

mío, your adopted nickname
mío con su bigote finó
tinted gray, touched by wisdom and age
his corner hairs make, perfect sea-shape
80% Vicente Fernandez,
a debonair gentleman
mexicano puro, 10% granjero
collection of chickens, pigs, cows, and horses
huevos dé la gallina, you taught me how to pick 'em
los nietos pedacitos de oro
i treasure you endlessly

abuelos maternos

my voice is worthy

listen | *escucha*

this is not my story

it is hers, her mothers, their daughters…

recollective memories, *cosas del pasado*

abuelo- educational level, first-grade| primer grado
|brick by brick|
built himself the title of architect

abuela- no employment verification, just years and years,

pura experiencia de vida

chef, niñera, consejera, estilista, y madre

much much more than everyday pay

<u>recipe for forgotten remnants of you</u>

| add ½ cup of love-the part i press & beg for |
| substitute heavy cream in lieu of passion |
| whisk in 2 tablespoons vanilla bean paste: the sweetness missing between us |
| blend again & again with too much confidence & a lifetime worth of "what if's" |
| drizzle in excuses |
      taste the bitterness of a one-sided love

grease monkey

my mechanic smells of diesel, sloshed all over his jumper uniform
my mechanic is the know-it-all of cars, knows them all, by make &
model

their unique,
      VROOOM....VROOM.... &
            BEEP.... BEEP ....

magical tools, sockets & ratchets
stripping bolts & other nonsense

      their roaring engines | bangin'& clangin'

my mechanic comes home lookin' rough
      grime & dirt meet his bushy eyebrows

my mechanic comes home with bruised knuckles
      & slashes across his hands

coal-black skin | thank you, manual labor

tattered clothes, they never last

easy come | easy go

<u>note to self: do not let people walk all over you</u>

red, hot, fiery madness, quivers
sends, striking shivers down my spine

  to the tops of my brain,
y'all motherfuckers drive me insane
   how many times do i have to bite my tongue?
   how many times do i have to repeat,
      & admit defeat?

   i will not let myself be beat

<u>hungry for change</u>

lunch and dinner spewed out of me
the taste of vomit became a daily flavor
one that I savored, mainly to contemplate her

"don't eat so much you'll mess up your figure!"

my mind was automatically triggered
she set her hopes and dreams through me
hoping i will do everything she didn't
and succeed

this disorder latched on to me past the age of seventeen
tooth- decaying, weight maintaining, iron cells deflating,
and affecting all that was left of me

<u>ASMR does not help me go to sleep</u>

insomnia creeps in at night

·

      anxiety embraces me by morning

·

      suicidal thoughts surge

·

by evening, i slither into this distressful isolation

·

      by the next day, it takes its toll on me like

demonic possession without permission to

enter my body

i need some time to think about my life

&

ponder

what is left for me to uncover, discover…

-adventure awaits

café por la mañana

una tácita
filled with this milky reflection
caramelo circula,
café de Folgers
té veo con tanta delicadeza
soft & cuddly |
pero tú piel
broken-down |
de tanto enfrentó qué has sobrevivido
cosas de las que no se hablan
sweet bread,
ripples of hot pink, *la concha*
you dip once
you dip twice
in your creamy
steamy concoction

#BodyShaming

when will we move past a world that insults
      the too skinny | *muy flacos*
      the too fat | *barrigón, pansón*
when will we meet in the middle

tus palabras, molding me like clay
i am tired of searching for those that made me feel beautiful
i want to be with people who float above criticisms
flee the common narrative
      gente valiente, sin miedo a nada

mi domicilio, on this planet, no es mi cuerpo

      it is my soul | *es mi alma*

<u>sometimes people just don't give a fuck</u>

do you care through all my despair
you can't understand what is unfair
so many fucking memories shared

                    tell me, i am more
                    tell me, you love me so…
                    tell me, how much i am worth
                    tell me, i am all you think at night
                    tell me, you will put up the fight
                    tell me, everything will be alright
                    tell me, i am the most beautiful sight

                    tell me…

<u>there is no place for our voice in México</u>

mute

shut those lips tight

anything we say may not be right

"y no hablen en Inglés, no pueden saber de dónde somos"

mama con piel oscurita, yo güerita

wetback stamped on my forehead

cada pie

equally planted

| Mexi-Americaricana |

you don't own me

remember, you have my heart, but i am not your possession

i am human | *carne y hueso*

remember, once, i was your obsession

i cared for you in those darkest hours, you fed & fed me with deception

recuérdame, porqué me enamoré de ti?

<u>tradiciones en la calle</u>

my dad's love language es viajar a Tamaulipas, almost every weekend /
i baptized him el máster
Valle Hermoso / el quiere tomar sus chelas / asar una fajita
los domingos / yo un border kid /
Duelo, Intocable, y Pesado a todo vuelo / steering wheel at
arm's length / gas station taquitos,
gobbled down, three bites or less / two bathroom breaks in the
timespan of 7 hours / gas pump
burps for more / la familia que te queda es lo qué buscas / familiarity,
ese es tú amor /

as a poet, i may have all the words on paper,
yet when it comes to you
there are
no words
they escape me
-@Crisreyeswrites

if the shoe fits

"well maybe not all of us got it good like you…"

this girl, ain't got no shame
girl, don't come at me with that game
       i've been
    the single mom
    the teen mom
    the homeless mom
    the "where do i go from here" mom
    the living off WIC benefits mom
    the look-up my food-stamps balance at midnight mom

        check here:
            [ ] single
            [ ] married
            [ ] widowed

        not single, nor halfway married, just girl meets boy,

                girl births kid to live in
                this world of misfortune

<u>WWWD: what would writers do?</u>

as a writer, you crave experience

        &

you value knowledge so that one day you merge the two,

        in an attempt to unleash a masterpiece

V

O

M I S S I N G

D

ode to breastfeeding

| liquid gold trickles |
all areola / nipple peeks /
you bathe in plump, gushy goodness

(.)   (.)
lips pressed / every swallow /
spread myself too thin / demand & command / milk flows /
split second, i see you grow /
| cuddle closer, i need your warmth |

my daughter's way of life

for Evelyn

i live for Taco Bell parking-lot banter
i live for our anime chats & non-stop laughter
i live for the times you teach me about TikTok & editing features
i live for the ultrasound i held at seventeen years old

you live from me & i live for you

<u>love take the wheel</u>

asi se siente / to drop everything /
stomach in knots / *sin voz* / *el amor me maneja*

<u>inclination</u>

i want a love so great it can

```
                    NT
              U        A
          O                  I
M O V E   M                      N
                                    S
```

it can alter our perceptions of the universe
a love we channel,
one-on-one gazes
telepathy
&
synchronicity
it will make us better and not bitter
it will not alter us but transform us

CRYSTAL REYES LOZANO

las mujeres de mí familia,
have carried me
embraced me in harsh moments
-@Crisreyeswrites

<u>life isn't always fair, but at least we got reggaeton</u>

| vas a llorar y batallar |

la vida
will throw you curveball after curveball
they will hit you with immense force
sweep you off your feet

| no te dejes por vencido |

como dice la bebecita, mañana será bonito

<u>ode to the creative writing professors</u>

quiero que sepan,   *me salvaron*
in my hit-fucking rock bottom moments
in my starless moments, *me salvaron*

a safe haven
an escape from reality
words crept in my brain;
laid out in spiral notebooks

d   e   s   o   r   d   e   n
alfabetico

algun momento solita
when heaviness outweighs the light
me acorde–   what is in sight

<u>not like the other kids</u>

for Luna

kids with multiple families,
you are not lended weekly,
but blended,
mezclados juntos
perhaps,
not your favorite recipe
we come together,
strengthened,
all hands on deck,
shared holidays
&
half-summers away,
double the hugs
&
quadruple the shoulders to lean on
you will never be loved less
this is our superpower;
this is your regular

termination station

chalky walls, concealed and obscure
jam-packed, lifeless women, shoulder to shoulder
the youngest clung to her mother, with worrisome eyes
a sought-out lawyer, middle-aged, hands clasped to her partners

conjoined for the task of endangering our own lives
to get rid of one that was unplanned
our shudders, kept us warm in thought
through the coldness of this act

faded from those medications
the ones that leave no flashbacks
not even a phantom of the pain demised
just the tingles of my vagina pulsating
embryonic knob detached
from the monstrosity i signed-off to

-places that still haunt my reality

<u>my teenage daughter does not know my sacrifices</u>

i may be "vintage" & not this generation's definition of hip &
cool / cool enough to be a teen mother at seventeen / seventeen
dollars i held onto from my sold off book collection / collection of
memorabilia tucked neatly away / away with all the societal stigmas
/ stigmas do not make or break me / me, the only thing i held onto,
as i fought to keep you close / close enough to protect you from the
outside / the outside, a place that knows the true me

naturalized citizen

red
white
&
green
lineage that reigns
serape sewn in my blood
nos mantine conecta2
crucified bodies
día por día
welcome to
AMERI-KKK-A
reina
rosario in hand
inhala la bendición
exhala la maldición

i am ~~bisexual~~ pansexual

i considered you a
fashion-forward icon
hiding underneath oversized t-shirts
& thrift shop, rocker-style boots

they.
a term i was familiar with,
but not so up close & personal
"i go by they/them pronouns"

i still feel them whispering their truth
it did not shock, nor bother me
it did not lessen my feelings
it did shift our love lives

<u>wild child</u>

reheated coffee buzzes for the fifth time
by day, the living room becomes my son's jungle gym
whirled with boundless energy
    i, on the other hand, hair knotted, listless attitude
ready for fri-yay, oh, but when does overtime kick-in for a mother?

    i find my friends, mingling in Montrose, a place once
    suitable
for slippery nipples & drunken make-out sessions with women
where i skip & sway all my worries away
    my own playground

fortunate

| feeling, craving, yearning, desire, impulse, need, itch, proclivity…

the ultimate yen

foundations that remind me, there is much more to life |

<u>mercury in gatorade or whatever these kids call it</u>

she is ruled by stubbornness & hard-headedness

determined | sensual creature

she is never wrong, seeks where to belong

down-to-earth | herbaceous florae

elements equally aligned,
fire, earth, air, & water

radiate divinity | cardenal energy

someone will love you, for you

my mom says,

"a man will not want you with one baby daddy, but you got two,
    so your chances are out the window!"

my inbox says otherwise

    &

    who said i was looking for a man?

impulsive

| sometimes,
 i wonder how i got so far away
           from the person i wanted to be,
                        for good reason i suppose |

           i enjoy the present me,
                        so much more

| sometimes,
 i wonder how i got so far away

postpartum mom

cinnamon dust fills my nostrils
flame on medium heat
nagging from the puberty-stricken teen
cries from the upset toddler
the other pulls on my insides & retracts to my ribs
& now, suddenly, i am a thirty-year-old parent
you would think the momma routine becomes simple,
quite effortless
yet we made it this far
while we wither in our physique:

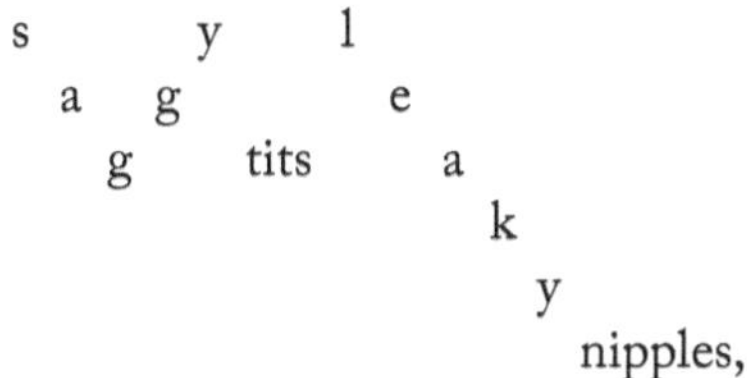

slouchy postpartum bellies scorned for not 'bouncing-back'
indented rough-patched streaks throughout my body
baby blues that were uninvited
but we manage to set this aside,
our happiness becomes
the enlivened sacred space,
they call home

madness

———————————————————

has sawed me in

———————————————

|two|

les encanta el chisme

mi madre chismosa,
  "¡Que gorda te ves!"

shames me once,
how my ass jiggles,
later, admires its ballon-like complex

mi madre chismosa,
  "¡Que caderas mijita!"

my hips as wide as the Rio Grande,
hechas y derechas,
perfect for baby birthing
gifted me, *tres bendiciones*

mamá says,
"pa' que te deprimes, tienes todo en la vida!"

she does not comprehend depression or mental health
i sometimes think she plays pretend

once i swallowed, *un arcoíris de pastillas*
my first attempt at suicide
zig-zag cuts marked here & there
mi madre knows nothing
de mi cuerpo,
nada de mi vida

who am i?

| i am stubborn and charismatic

    picosa y poderosa

i wonder why i was always labeled,

    'la oveja negra'

me encanta, la voz de mi abuela, soft & kind-spoken

i close my eyes,

    veo girasoles, yellow baby suns trailed all around me

i want to leave behind written memories; *palabras que impactan*

    yo soy madre, hija, guerrera; i pretend to be as tough as rocks

    yo siento que no todos me comprenden

i am capable of making all my dreams come true

i worry about the future *y las cosas que son fuera de mi control*

i cry when i don't succeed *y lloró por que siento mucho* |

<u>angel number</u>

if magic is what you are looking for

    magic is what you will find

        [manifest]
        [manifest]
        [manifest]

<u>greñuda</u>

madre hates her hair, *le grita al espejo "estas greñas gruesas"*
       leaves me legacy
              corkscrew curls
     unmanageable
gel does not settle in
       does not tame
i stick to mom's hair formula
       lactescent mousse
           crinkles
crunch & munch
       no longer a fragment of myself

full moons are for rebirth

luna llena,

she glimmers luminescence
          through darkness

la oscuridad canta,

drunken starry night,
          lulls me tender*ly*

<u>calypso</u>

i like to think of myself,
as a beautiful disaster
turbulent & cataclysmic

not the calm after a storm
or the
"things will get better in due time"

my mood masks the atmosphere
all gloom & doom
i whorl into wildness

| we hide what others do not approve |

•

| *ocultamos lo que otros no aprueban* |

-@Crisreyeswrites

<u>modern mothers</u>

1. mothers aren't supposed to dress-up or look sexy
       my sexy is slacks & blazers
2. mothers should stay home & cook for their spouses
       my man knows how to order UberEats
3. mothers do not have a life outside of their kids
       my ideal date is coffee & pistachio croissants at Common Bond
4. mothers are superwomen, they can do it all
       my superpower is sticky note reminders & caffeine

---

road rage   road rage   road rage   road rage

tortura

alomejor es la soledad que te llama,
pero desde qué te conocí no paró de pensar en ti
alomejor es la soledad que te llama,
pero desde qué te conocí no paró de pensar en ti
alomejor es la soledad que te llama,
pero desde qué te conocí no paró de pensar en ti
alomejor es la soledad que te llama,
pero desde qué te conocí no paró de pensar en ti
alomejor es la soledad que te llama,
pero desde qué te conocí no paró de pensar en ti
alomejor es la soledad que te llama,
pero desde qué te conocí no paró de pensar en ti
alomejor es la soledad que te llama,
pero desde qué te conocí no paró de pensar en ti
alomejor es la soledad que te llama,
pero desde qué te conocí no paró de pensar en ti
alomejor es la soledad que te llama,
pero desde qué te conocí no paró de pensar en ti
alomejor es la soledad que te llama,
pero desde qué te conocí no paró de pensar en ti

drunk on heartache

falling in love makes me weak
i lose all senses, even the ability to speak
vulnerability slathers
heart-still beating

<u>ámate un poco</u>

espero que tengan esos días /

los que te quitan la respiración /

que tienes que respirar profundamente /

para realizar lo especial que realmente eres

some opportunities are like shooting stars,

you have to catch them while you can

-@Crisreyeswrites

<u>unchained</u>

in my hands i hold history
tangled furry
resentment hides
unshackled mind

[too free for this world]